Discovering

FRESHWATER FISH

Bernice Brewster

Illustrations by Vanda Baginska.

Discovering Nature

Discovering Ants
Discovering Bees and Wasps
Discovering Beetles
Discovering Birds of Prey
Discovering Butterflies and Moths
Discovering Crabs and Lobsters
Discovering Crickets and Grasshoppers
Discovering Damselflies and Dragonflies
Discovering Ducks and Geese
Discovering Flies

Discovering Flowering Plants
Discovering Freshwater Fish
Discovering Frogs and Toads
Discovering Fungi
Discovering Hedgehogs
Discovering Otters
Discovering Rabbits and Hares
Discovering Rats and Mice
Discovering Sea Birds
Discovering Slugs and Snails
Discovering Snakes and Lizards
Discovering Spiders
Discovering Squirrels
Discovering Worms

Further titles are in preparation

First published in 1987 by
Wayland (Publishers) Limited
61 Western Road, Hove
East Sussex BN3 1JD, England

© Copyright 1987 Wayland (Publishers) Limited

British Library Cataloguing in Publication Data
Brewster, Bernice
    Discovering freshwater fish.—
    (Discovering nature).
    1. Fishes, Fresh-water—Juvenile
    literature
    I. Title   II. Series
    597.092'9   QL624

ISBN 1–85210–062–1

Typeset by DP Press Limited, Sevenoaks, Kent
Printed and Bound in Italy by Sagdos S.p.A., Milan

Editor: Clare Chandler

All photographs from Oxford Scientific Films

Cover *The perch lives in lowland lakes, ponds and slow-flowing rivers.*

Frontispiece *The carp feeds in weedy waters on the bottom of lakes and rivers.*

Contents

1
Introducing Fish

This cichlid is a typical freshwater fish. It is found in Africa and South America.

What is a Fish?

There are about 22,000 different kinds of fish, but only 6,900 or so that live in fresh water; the rest live in the sea.

Fish usually swim by powerful body muscles – so what do fins do? The dorsal and anal fins each work like a keel on a boat so the fish cannot roll from side to side while swimming. The tail fin works like a rudder on a boat and steers the fish through the water. The pectoral and pelvic fins control fine movements of the fish.

To help **bony fish** float in the water, they have an air-filled sac called a swimbladder inside their bodies. The amount of air in the swimbladder is controlled by the fish. If air is added, the fish rises and if air is removed, the fish sinks.

The outside of a fish's body is covered in thin bony plates called scales. On each side of a fish's body there is a row of scales each of which has a small hole, or pore, in the centre. These pores lead to a thin tube beneath the skin called the lateral line. This has special sense cells which help the fish to feel movements in the water nearby.

Right *The pike is common in the colder regions of the northern hemisphere.*

PARTS OF A FISH

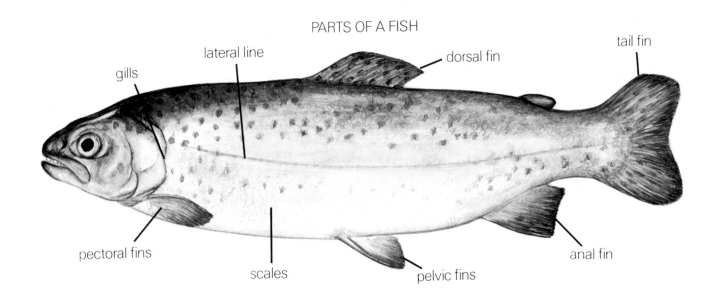

gills

lateral line

dorsal fin

tail fin

pectoral fins

scales

pelvic fins

anal fin

Fresh Water

Fresh water, unlike sea water, does not contain any salt and has only a few minerals.

European lakes tend to be rather quiet and large **shoals** of minnows are often found at the water's edge. However, the great lakes of Africa are

A typical jungle stream where fish such as neon tetras, catfish, and cichlids live.

immense and very deep, and each has its own kind of cichlid fish living in it. A number of Nile perch were put into Lake Victoria, about twenty years ago. They are large **predatory** fish and have increased in such large numbers that they have now eaten all the cichlid fish.

In Europe and North America, streams and rivers tend to be clear and well- oxygenated. Where waters pass through farmland, cattle and sheep drink the water and make small, deep pools where their feet have sunk in the mud at the water's edge. These pools make ideal nurseries for baby fish where they are safe from being eaten by other kinds of fish.

Electric fish such as the electric eel, are commonly found in murky waters like those of the **black rivers** of tropical South America. Their eyesight is poor and they rely on sending out electric pulses which bounce off objects in the water back towards the fish. Special receptors in the skin pass this information to the brain which gives the fish an electrical picture. Such fish also 'talk' to each other using electric signals.

The water in an **estuary** can vary from very salty to almost fresh water. Some fish can live in this changing **habitat**, for example flounders, which are a kind of flatfish.

The flounder lives in estuaries. Look carefully at the eyes and mouth – both eyes are on the same side of its head.

Fresh Water and the Sea

Most freshwater fish can only live in salt-free water and would quickly die if put into sea water or even into an estuary.

A few fish can pass from the sea to fresh water and back again. The best-known fish to make this journey is the salmon. The salmon **migrates** from the sea to **spawn** many miles inland, in gravelly shallows where the water flows rapidly and is ideal for the eggs to hatch in. The young salmon leave the freshwater spawning site and travel to the sea where they grow up.

Eels spawn in the mid Atlantic Ocean, in an area called the Sargasso Sea. The young eels are flattened and transparent; looking very different from their parents and after about two

A salmon leaping a waterfall in Alaska on its way to spawn.

Young eels that have been netted on their way upstream from the sea.

months, when they are only 2.5 cm long, they drift in the **Gulf Stream** towards Europe. The journey takes about two and a half years for the small eels to reach the coasts of Europe. Whilst in the coastal waters, these young eels **metamorphose** into **elvers** before migrating into rivers, where they feed and grow. The male eel stays in fresh water for between 5–10 years, the female stays there up to 20 years before returning to the sea to make her long spawning migration.

How Fish Breathe

Like all animals, fish need to breathe oxygen, but unlike **terrestrial** animals which breathe oxygen in the air, fish have to use the oxygen in the water. To do this, they pump water through their bright red **gills**. On one side of each gill arch are fine filaments that are richly supplied with blood to

The Siamese fighting fish lives in poorly oxygenated water, so, as well as gills, it has an organ for breathing air at the surface.

take the oxygen out of the water. On the other side of the gill are fleshy bumps called gill rakers which stop large particles in the water from damaging the gill filaments. The gills are protected by a large flat bone called the operculum.

By breathing air, some fish manage to live in stagnant water which has very little oxygen in it. As the lungfish which lives in African lakes has very small gills, it gulps air at the surface, then 'swallows' it into its swim-bladder through an opening in the gullet. The swimbladder acts as a lung and oxygen is absorbed by its walls.

Some catfish live in shallow streams and pools in Africa and Asia. During the dry season, these temporary waters dry up and the catfish must migrate in search of new water to survive. They have a fleshy, branched organ inside their bodies which they use to breathe oxygen whilst out of the water, so they can wriggle quite long distances to another stream.

A catfish wriggling across the mud to find another pond.

Other Senses

Just like humans, fish can see, smell, taste, hear and feel, but one or other of these senses may be better developed according to the type of life they lead. Most predatory fish have very good eyesight so they can hunt and catch their prey.

The eyes of fish are similar to our own, except that fish do not need eyelids because the surface of the eye is kept clean and moist by the water.

Although fish cannot close their eyes, they do sleep, often resting on the bottom or against a water plant.

Some fish live in pools deep inside caves, which are so dark that they have lost their eyes and are blind. The skin over the whole body is very sensitive, so that they can feel their way around.

All fish have nostrils, which are not used for breathing but for smelling. The nostrils are deep pits, lined with special skin which is sensitive to

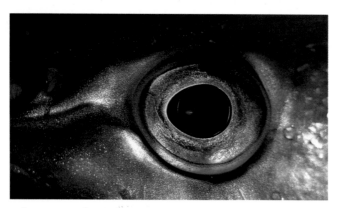

The eye of a pike. Can you see the two nostrils on the left?

This perch is sleeping although its eyes are open. Fish do not have eyelids.

water-borne smells. Most fish have four nostrils on their snouts, but some have two, and the lampreys have only one which is on the top of their heads!

Fish can sample the water and their food with taste buds. These are not just on the tongue but may be on the outside of the head or even on the fins and body.

Although fish do not have ears like ours, they can hear. The ears are

Gudgeon push their tentacles between stones to taste for something good to eat.

generally rather simple and their hearing is poor. Catfish and carp-like fish have special bones on the fronts and top of their backbones that improve their ability to hear. A number of these kinds of fish also make noises, so that they can 'talk' to each other.

2
Food and Feeding

The piranha is the most ferocious freshwater fish. It has sharp inter-locking teeth for tearing apart its prey.

Eating Other Fish

Many fish eat animals of some kind. The majority of predatory fish hunt alone but the piranha hunt in shoals. They live in the jungle rivers and streams of South America. Each piranha has powerful jaws armed with a row of razor-sharp teeth. When they attack a fish, they strip it of flesh in seconds. Piranha are attracted to splashing and noise. The lateral line can sense the movements of prey in the water and piranha have very acute hearing.

Pike and pickerels – well known in Europe and North America – also eat other fish. Their greenish striped and speckled coloration makes them invisible amongst the weeds where they lurk. Pike hunt by sight, keeping very still and then springing out from their hiding places to snatch up passing fish. They can grow very large;

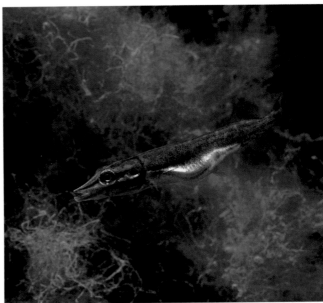

This pike has caught a smaller pike which it has swallowed whole.

a big pike can easily weigh 22.7 kg. Garpikes are solitary hunters that live in the rivers of North America. Their bodies are similar in shape to the pikes but the jaws are very long and armed with lots of uneven teeth, making them look like crocodiles. The garpike seeks a shoal of fish and floats towards them looking just like a drifting log. Once amongst them, the garpike suddenly jerks its head to one side biting one of the fish before swallowing it whole.

The perch is smaller than either the pike or garpike. Although usually in shoals, each fish hunts alone, darting out from weeds to catch fish smaller than itself, including its own young.

Eating Insects

Fish that eat insects rely on their eyesight to see their prey on the water surface. The water in which these fish live is usually crystal clear. Some kinds of fish eat insects in the water. The North American darters are so named because of their habit of darting between stones where they

This pike is stalking a dragonfly nymph.

feed on insect larvae in the water.

Trout and salmon are fast, powerful swimmers and are usually seen

This archer fish is just about to shoot the insect off the leaf.

quietly cruising around the rocks and stones at the bottom of the river. When insects or flies land on the water, they zoom up and snatch them off the surface, sometimes coming up so fast they actually leap out. Rudd swim just below the surface and snap up insects as they land on the water. The rudd has no teeth in its mouth but chews up the insects with big, sharp teeth at the back of its throat.

Perhaps the most unusual insect eater is the archer fish which lives in murky waters of Asia. It spits drops of water with great force at its insect prey. It has a special groove in the roof of its mouth, into which the tongue fits to form a narrow tube. When the archer fish spots a juicy insect on a bankside plant, it shoots drops of water through the tube at great speed and with enough force to knock the insect into the water. It can shoot down an insect at a distance of 1.5 m.

Eating Plants

Plants are found in abundance growing in and around water. Many kinds of fish eat plants as well as insect larvae and **crustaceans**, but there are very few fish that eat only plants. Plants alone are not very nutritious unless huge amounts of them are eaten.

The grass carp feeds only on vegetation. It is a large fish, weighing up to 32 kg, with a cylindrical body and broad head with a large mouth. It bites pieces off the plants with its hard-skinned lips, then chews them

The common carp eats water plants and insects. It chews its food with teeth that are in the back of its throat.

up with large teeth in the back of the throat. The grass carp lives in lowland rivers of China but has been introduced to parts of Europe, Russia, America and England to eat water weeds clogging canals and reservoirs. In Asia, the grass carp is important as a food fish. It is cheap to keep because it thrives on a diet of vegetable waste such as grass clippings.

The sucking loach, or Siamese algal eater, has lips which are hard and

These sucking loach are eating the algae on the stone. Can you see the fleshy suckers holding them on to the stone?

ridged to that it can scrape algae, which are very small plants, growing on rocks and stones. Just underneath the chin it has a fleshy organ which enables it to 'suck' on to rocks and stones. This stops it from being swept away while feeding in the fast flowing streams where it lives.

3
Reproduction

This female three-spined stickleback is being courted by the brightly-coloured male.

Breeding

The time of the breeding season depends mostly on the weather and the amount of food available to the baby fish. In Europe and North America, the majority of fish breed in the spring and summer when the water is warmer than in the cold winter months. Throughout spring and summer, there are plenty of insects, crustaceans, tadpoles, other young fish and plants to be found, so there are lots of different kinds of food for the baby fish. In parts of Africa which become very dry and dusty, many kinds of fish, such as some catfish, breed in the rainy season so there is no risk of pools and ponds drying out and killing the young.

During the breeding season, female fish rarely change much in appearance apart from becoming plumper due to the formation of eggs in their bodies, but males often become more colourful and active at this time. This coloration is to attract females, but drive off other males. Male roach, rudd, carp and minnow grow hard, wart-like pimples called breeding tubercles on their heads and often on their backs and sides as well. The breeding tubercles may help in fighting rival males, or in stimulating females to lay eggs when nudged by the warty males' heads. The male minnow also has a bright red belly, a dramatic change from its usual yellow-white colour.

This blue male Siamese fighting fish is enticing the female to lay her eggs.

Laying Eggs

Fish eggs are usually quite small, the larger ones being only 1–2 mm in diameter. They are filled with a rich yolk that the babies feed on, even when hatched.

Many fish scatter their eggs on the leaves of water plants. Others scoop out gravel with their bodies and tails to form shallow pits in which to deposit their eggs. Large numbers of males and females gather together and the females begin laying their eggs which are fertilized as the males

The female trout is laying her eggs in the gravel and the male is fertilizing them.

shed their **sperm** into the water. Some fish build nests in which to lay eggs. It is the male who makes the nest and often looks after the eggs as well. The three-spined stickleback male constructs a nest from pieces of plant. He spreads a sticky substance produced in his kidneys over the plant material to hold it together. Once a small pile has been stuck together, he burrows through the middle to make a tunnel and complete the nest. The male then courts a **gravid** female, enticing her into the nest to lay her eggs; once she has left, the male enters and **fertilizes** them.

Bitterlings lay their eggs in a very unusual place, inside a freshwater mussel. The female bitterling has a 5 cm fleshy tube attached to the anal fin. It is not known whether the eggs pass down this tube or if the female uses it to 'tickle' the mussel so that it does not snap its shell shut before she

This is a nest built by the male ten-spined stickleback. Look carefully to see the eggs in the middle of the nest.

has laid her eggs. The male bitterling sheds his sperms in the mussel's 'mouth' so that they are sucked in as the mussel breathes and the eggs are fertilized.

4
Growing Up

The baby trout that has hatched is still attached to a large yolk sac, which you can see just below its head.

Surviving Alone

Most fish have nothing more to do with their eggs once they have been laid and fertilized. Lampreys spawn on gravelly river beds in spring. The adults dig a shallow nest in the gravel in which the eggs are laid and fertilized. It takes about ten to fifteen days for the lamprey **larvae** to hatch. The larvae are worm-like, blind and toothless, feeding on microscopic plants and animals. They stay at the nest site for about another thirty days before swimming downstream to a suitable spot where the river bottom is of soft sand or mud where they bury themselves.

Trout spawn in gravelly shallows in the winter. It takes about two months for the baby fish to develop and they hatch in early spring. The young trout spend their first two or three weeks of life near the nest feeding on insects and their larvae. Gradually, as the young fish grow they move away from the nest into deeper waters. Some kinds of trout swim out to sea when they are about one year old and spend from six months to five years feeding on the rich supplies of **invertebrates** and small fish to be found there. They are called sea trout, but like salmon, they return to rivers to spawn.

Pike spawn in early spring, and the eggs are scattered on bankside plants.

Roach and rudd spawn in spring and summer in shallow weedy areas of rivers. After hatching, the young form large shoals in quiet shallows around the edge of the river, while the parents live in the mainstream.

These baby roach are swimming in very shallow water, where they are safe from bigger fish which would eat them.

Parental Care

Those fish which do not care for their young lay thousands of eggs each time they breed. However, the few kinds which care for their eggs and young lay only hundreds of eggs, because they protect them from predators, so more of the babies survive.

As soon as the female three-spined stickleback has laid her eggs she swims away and has nothing else to do with them. After fertilizing the eggs, the male defends the nest. From time to time he **aerates** the eggs with fanning movements of his pectoral fins, and once the eggs hatch, he guards the young. If one strays from the rest, he chases after it, and carrying it in his mouth returns it to its brothers and sisters.

Some female cichlids protect their eggs by carrying them in their mouths. Even when hatched, the youngsters stay in her mouth until they are several days old. When they get bigger, the young fish leave the female but if danger threatens, they rapidly return to the shelter of her mouth. The female does not feed while brooding her young.

The discus fish lives in the rivers of South America. When the young hatch, they feed on the slime covering the bodies of the parents.

This male three-spined stickleback is aerating the developing eggs in his nest.

The splashing tetra lays its eggs on leaves out of the water where they are safe from other predatory fish. The male leads a gravid female to leaves overhanging the water and jumps up to them. The female then jumps up clinging on to the leaf just long enough to lay a few eggs which the male then leaps up to fertilize. For about three days the male swims just below the leaf with the eggs, splashing water over them until they hatch. Once the youngsters fall off the leaf into the water, the male's parental activities are over.

Some cichlid fish protect their eggs and babies inside their mouths.

Live Bearers

The guppy and a number of its relatives give birth to live young. In these fish, the eggs are fertilized inside the body of the female. The male guppy's anal fin is used to transfer sperm to the female. Internal fertilization of the eggs is another way of ensuring the 20–30 youngsters are protected until they are born. Once the female guppy has been **mated**, the sperm is released very slowly so that several generations of young can be produced from one mating. The fertilized eggs develop in the female's egg cavity, the growing babies feeding on the yolk. The female gives birth to the young whilst they are still enclosed in an egg **membrane** which bursts immediately they are born.

The male guppy is brightly coloured and smaller than the pregnant female.

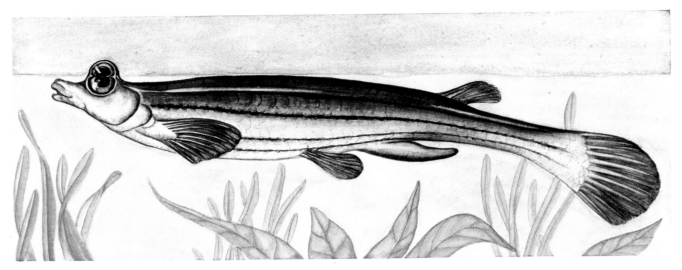

The Amazon molly lives in Texas and Mexico. It is a very unusual kind of fish because it only consists of female populations. The Amazon mollies 'mate' with males of related species but although the sperm does not fertilize the eggs, its presence makes the baby fish develop. Like the guppy, the young are born live.

The four-eyed fish live in Southern Mexico and northern South America. Each eye is divided into an upper and lower half. They always have the tops

The four-eyed fish can watch for prey above and below the water at the same time.

of their heads and eyes out of the water because the top part of the eye can see things on the land and in the air, whilst the bottom part can see under water. The fertilized eggs of the four-eyed fish develop inside the female's body but unlike the guppy, the babies do not feed on yolk but are fed by an organ which absorbs nutrients from the mother.

5
Fish Bred for a Purpose

The eggs of the female trout are gently squeezed out. They will then be fertilized with sperm from a male trout.

Fish Bred for Food

Fish are a very important food, so some kinds are bred especially for this purpose. Some, such as trout, are considered to be a delicacy and are commercially farmed, particularly in Europe and America. The farms have a number of adult males and females called the brood stock. These are mated; the resulting eggs and young fish are then looked after by the farmer. In the wild, fish only breed at certain times of the year, but the fish farmers can change the conditions in which their brood fish live and always have some in breeding condition. Fish farming is very important in parts of the world such as Africa and Asia, where there is a shortage of meat.

Two kinds of trout are farmed, the brown and rainbow trout. The ripe eggs are gently squeezed out of a gravid female and sperm from the male is run onto them by pressing his belly. The fertilized eggs are spread on large water-covered trays and carefully **incubated**. When the young are about 2.5 cm in length they are transferred to large ponds.

In many European countries, eels are a very popular food. Eels cannot be properly farmed because they only spawn in the Sargasso Sea and cannot be bred in captivity. To overcome this problem, eel farmers catch the elvers every year as they migrate up river in large shoals.

Rainbow trout like this are popular food fish. They originated in North America but are now common throughout Europe.

Fish Bred for Stock

In Europe and America, some fish are bred specially for re-stocking lakes and rivers. The kinds of fish used for re-stocking are those that occur naturally, for example in Britain, roach, rudd, bream, chub and barbel are bred for this purpose. When the fish in a river have been killed by pollution, restocking with certain kinds of fish is necessary once the water is clean again. Sometimes fish are stocked in places such as reservoirs or old quarry workings that have filled with water. Anglers are also keen to have fishing waters stocked with plenty of their favourite kinds of fish. Re-stocking can also be important for conservation. In America, the desert pupfish which is a close relation of the guppy, is almost extinct in the wild. These fish are now being bred in captivity. When there

are enough, some will be released into rivers in the wild, where, it is hoped, they will start breeding naturally and increase their numbers again.

In Europe, the roach is one of the easiest fish to breed for re-stocking. The babies are usually kept until they

Chub such as this one are often bred in captivity and their young re-introduced into suitable habitats in the wild.

are about one year old and quite big before being put into water where they must fend for themselves. In the wild, roach will **hybridise** with rudd, bream and chub. So, to keep the stock of these fish pure, the adults must be examined carefully before breeding.

The bream has been re-stocked in the wild and is a favourite catch for anglers.

6
Enemies of Fish

Kingfishers are just one of the many birds that feed on fish.

Enemies of Fish

There are lots of animals that will catch fish if they can, including humans. Anglers find it a great challenge to tempt fish into eating some delicacy which also disguises a nasty hook. Many anglers return the fish to the water, but some fish are very tasty and end up being eaten.

One of the main predators of fish are birds. Kingfishers patiently wait on a branch overhanging water and then, with an amazing turn of speed, dive into the water to catch a fish. Birds such as dippers and cormorants that swim on the water surface and dive after fish, can spend several minutes under water chasing them. In tropical areas there are also many animals that stalk fish.

Some kinds of lamprey **parasitize** other fish. They swim up to a fish and attach themselves to it by means of their circular mouths and big teeth. The lamprey slowly rasps off the skin, and the muscle from the fish at the site where it is attached. When it has finished feeding, the lamprey drops off. The damage caused by the lamprey usually heals but sometimes if the **host** fish is already sick or weak, it dies from the wound.

Leeches are also a hazard to fishes. The leech pierces the fish's skin with its mouthparts and injects a fluid that stops the blood clotting, then it sucks up the fish's blood. Usually leeches do not seriously injure a fish but if several catch the same one and start feeding, they can make the fish very ill.

This lamprey is feeding on a trout, rasping off the skin and muscle with its teeth.

7
Keeping Fish as Pets

This scissortail rasbora lives in Asia but is a very popular aquarium fish.

Tropical Fish

Keeping tropical fish as pets is becoming increasingly popular.

When starting to keep tropical fish it is important to buy the tank, gravel, plants, heater, filter and pump and set the tank up for about one week before putting in the fish. This allows the plants to root in the gravel, the water to settle and the temperature to be regulated at 23°C (74°F).

The aquarists' shop that sells the fish will have packed them in plastic bags. As tropical fish are very sensitive to changes in temperature, it is important to float the bags containing the fish in the tank for at least half an hour before releasing them. This allows the water in the bag to slowly reach the same temperature as that of the tank, avoiding giving the fish a shock which might kill them.

One of the best and prettiest

Neon tetras are very easy to keep in aquaria and will also breed in captivity.

aquarium fishes for the beginner are the neon tetras. These little fish come from the rivers of South America where they live in large shoals and so in aquaria are best kept in numbers of about a dozen.

Little is known about many tropical fish that appear for sale, so no one knows how to breed them in captivity. As a result, many are caught from where they live in the rivers of South America and Asia. But sadly, the majority of them die of shock or disease before ever reaching the aquarists' shop. This is a great cause for concern amongst conservation organizations such as the World Wildlife Fund and the Fauna and Flora Preservation Society who are trying to encourage the South American and Asian dealers to breed the tropical fish. Unless they are successful, it is probable that many kinds of these exploited tropical fish will become **extinct**.

neon tetra pond plants

heater

angel fish

filter and pump

oscar gravel rocks

Tropical fish need a heater in the aquarium to keep them at a constant temperature.

Goldfish and Koi

The goldfish is probably amongst the most popular of pets, only needing a daily pinch of food and the occasional change of cold water when kept in an aquarium. Goldfish are closely related to the carp and were originally bred in China.

Various strains of carp known as koi have been carefully bred from the common carp for their colour. The Japanese are renowned for the koi carp which they have been rearing for many hundreds of years. Except for their colour, koi carp look like the common variety but their bodies may be orange, white, orange and black, orange and white or even a mixture of all three colours. These strains of carp are popular and often very expensive.

The goldfish bowl is not a suitable home for fish; because of the bowl's shape, the water rapidly loses its oxygen and the fish are in danger of suffocating. It is best to keep goldfish in a rectangular tank, with lots of gravel on the bottom so that water plants can root in it and give the fish somewhere to hide. Often the goldfish will eat the plants in addition to their food. It is a good idea when keeping any fish in aquaria to have a small electric pump to supply air to the tank so that the water always has plenty of oxygen in it.

Goldfish and koi are often kept in garden ponds. Here the main problem is protecting the fish from local cats, but if there are a lot of water plants, the fish can hide in them.

Koi carp are popular pond fish throughout the world.

Glossary

Aerate To circulate air around.

Black rivers Dark rivers full of dead jungle plants, which contain few nutrients.

Bony fish Fish which have skeletons of bone.

Crustacean Animals with a hard shell, including crabs, shrimps and water fleas.

Elvers Young eels that are immature miniatures of the adults.

Estuary The wide mouth of a river where it meets the sea.

Evolved A gradual change in body form.

Extinct A group of animals or plants that have died out; for example, dinosaurs.

Fertilizes Joining the sperm with the egg, so that a new individual can grow.

Gills The branched or feather-like structures used for breathing under water.

Gravid A female that has ripe eggs and is ready to lay them.

Gulf Stream A warm surface ocean current that flows in the Atlantic Ocean.

Habitat Area in which an animal or plant lives.

Host An animal or plant on which a parasite feeds.

Hybridise A cross mating of related kinds of fish.

Incubated Kept warm. Eggs must be kept warm so that the baby fish can develop.

Invertebrate Creatures, like spiders and insects, which do not have backbones.

Larva (plural larvae) The form of an insect that emerges from the egg.

Mate The way in which male and female animals join together so that the female's eggs are fertilized by the male's sperm.

Membrane A thin skin around the egg.

Metamorphose A change in structure during the development of an animal after it has been hatched.

Migrate To move from one habitat to another at a particular time each year.

Parasitize To live and feed on another animal.

Predatory Catching and eating other animals.

Shoals Large groups of fish.

Spawn The act of laying eggs in water.

Sperm Male sex cells.

Terrestrial Living on land.

Finding Out More

If you would like to find out more about freshwater fish, you could read the following books:

N. Teitler, *The T.F.H. Book of Goldfish.* (T.F.H. Publications, 1981)

A. Wheeler, *The World Encyclopaedia of Fishes.* (Macdonald, 1984).

W. White, Jr., *The Guppy: Its Life Cycle.* (Sterling, 1974).

W. White, Jr., *The Siamese Fighting Fish: Its Life Cycle.* (Sterling, 1975).

Index

Picture acknowledgements

Photographs from Oxford Scientific Films by:

M. Austerman (Earth Scenes) 42; G.I. Bernard 11, 20, 21, 22, 27; Liz & Tony Bomford 31; Michael Fogden 10; Peter Gathercole 8, 19 (left & right), 23, 32, 34; Roger Jackman 18; Breck Kent (Animals Animals) 28, 35; Zig Leszczynski 41; Colin Milkins *frontispiece*; I.G. Moar 13; Peter Parks 26; J.E. Phling 39; Avril Ramage *cover*; Peter Stone 36; Stouffer Produtions Ltd (Animals Animals) 12; David Thompson 16 (left and right), 24, 29, 30, 37; G.M. Thompson 14, 25, 40; Barry Walker 38; P & W Ward 15; Illustrations by Vanda Baginska.